The investigations

Background inform

The start of each investigation contains a box like this.

Possible question

This question is a suggested starting point for your investigation. You will need to adapt the question to suit the things that interest you.

Possible hypothesis

This is only a suggestion. Don't worry if your hypothesis doesn't match the one listed here. Use your imagination!

Approximate cost of materials

Discuss this with your parents before starting work. Don't spend too much.

Materials needed

Make sure you can easily get all of the materials listed and gather them together before starting work. You could ask to borrow some items from school or from your parents.

Level of difficulty

There are three levels of investigations in this book: Easy, Intermediate, and Advanced. The level of difficulty is based on how long the investigation takes and how complicated it is.

1) How old is the resource? Is the information up to date or is it very old?

2) Who wrote the resource? Is the author identified so you know who they are, and what qualifies them to write about the topic?

3) What is the purpose of the resource? A website from a business or pressure group might not give balanced information, but one from a university probably will.

4) Is the information well documented? Can you tell where the author got their information from so you can check how accurate it is?

Some websites allow you to "chat" online with experts. Make sure you discuss this with a parent or teacher first. Never give out personal information online. The "Think U Know" website at http://www.thinkuknow.co.uk has loads of tips about safety online.

Once you know a little more about the subject you want to investigate, you'll be ready to work out your scientific question. You will be able to use this to make a sensible **hypothesis**. A hypothesis is an idea about why something happens that can be tested by doing experiments. Finally, you'll be ready to begin your science investigation!

This giant Ferris wheel is an example of a simple machine called a wheel and axle.

What is an experiment?

Often when someone says that they are going to do an experiment, they mean they are just going to fiddle with something to see what happens. But scientists mean something else. They mean that they are going to control the **variables** involved in a careful way. A variable is something that changes or can be changed. Independent variables are things that you deliberately keep the same or change in your experiment. You should always aim to keep all the independent variables constant, except for the one you are investigating. The dependent variable is the change that happens because of the one independent variable that you do change. You make a fair test if you set up your experiment so that you only change one independent variable at a time. Your results are valid if you have carried out a fair test, and recorded your results or observations honestly.

Often you need a **control** to test an idea against. Imagine you want to test whether the temperature of a liquid affects its ability to overcome **friction**. You could measure the amount of **effort** needed to move a heavy box over a surface covered with cooking oil that is at room temperature. Then you do the same procedure using both warmer and cooler cooking oil. Cooking oil at room temperature is your control. You would be looking to see if there is a difference between the control results and the results with oil at different temperatures. In this experiment, the temperature of the cooking oil is the independent variable, and the effort required to move the box is the dependent variable.

You must do experiments carefully so that your results are accurate and reliable. Ideally, you would get the same results if you did your investigation all over again.

Your hypothesis

Once you've decided on the question you're going to try to answer, you then make a scientific **prediction** of what you'll find out in your science project.

For example, if you wonder why some sailing boats use a system of pulleys to hoist their sails, your question might be, "Do pulleys make it easier to lift sails?" Remember, a hypothesis is an idea about why something happens, which can be tested by doing experiments. So your hypothesis in response to the above question might be, "The number of pulleys affects how much effort it takes to hoist the sails." With a hypothesis, you can also work out if you can actually do the experiments needed to answer your question. Think of a question like: "How many machines are there in the world?" It would be impossible to support your hypothesis, however you express it. This is because you can't possibly count all of the machines in the world. So, be sure you can actually get the **evidence** needed to support or disprove your hypothesis.

Keeping records

Good scientists keep careful notes in their lab book about everything they do. This is really important. Other scientists may want to try out the experiments to see if they get the same results. So the records in your lab book need to be clear and easy to follow. What sort of things should you write down?

It is a good idea to write some notes about the research you found in books and on websites. You should also include the names of the books or the web addresses. This will save you from having to find these useful resources all over again later. You should also write down your hypothesis and your reasons for it. All your **data** and results should go into your lab book, too.

Your results are the evidence that you use to make your conclusion. Never rub out an odd-looking result or tweak it to "look right". An odd result may turn out to be important later. You should write down *every* result you get. Tables are a really good way to record lots of results clearly. Make sure you record when you did your experiments, and anything you might have changed along the way to improve them. No detail is too small when it comes to scientific research.

There are tips for making a great report with each investigation and at the end of this book. Use them as guides and don't be afraid to be creative. Make it *your* investigation!

Quit the friction

Friction is a force that prevents an object from moving. It can cause you to increase the amount of force needed to move something, such as a heavy desk or a box of books. Fortunately, there are ways to decrease friction. Which way works best? Try this experiment to find out.

Do your research

Friction is a force that causes two objects to resist movement against each other. This force is usually measured in **newtons** (N). In this experiment, you will work with materials that reduce friction, called **lubricants.** Check with an adult about an appropriate place to use the lubricants so that children and pets are safe. Also, make sure the project space is well ventilated. Before you begin this project, do some research on friction and units of measurement. Once you've done some research, you can slide into doing this project. Or, you may come up with your own unique project after you've read and learned more about the topic.

Background information

Possible question

Which materials reduce friction the best?

Possible hypothesis

Oil-based materials are best at reducing friction.

Level of difficulty

Intermediate

Approximate cost of materials

£10.00

Materials needed

» Old newspapers » A hole punch
» A new baking tray with sides on it to contain the lubricants
» A 1-litre (1.8-pint) plastic storage container
» A spring scale that measures to 5 newtons
» 230 grams (8 ounces) sand
» 60 millilitres (2 fluid ounces) water
» 60 millilitres (2 fluid ounces) vegetable oil
» 60 millilitres (2 fluid ounces) dish soap

Here are some books and websites you could start with in your research:

» *Friction and Resistance*, Chris Oxlade (Heinemann Library, 2006)
» *Experiments with Friction*, Salvatore Tocci (Childrens Press, 2002)
» BBC: Schools: Science clips: Friction: http://www.bbc.co.uk/schools/scienceclips/ages/8_9/friction.shtml
» Energy, forces, and motion: Friction: http://www.darvill.clara.net/enforcemot/friction.htm

Outline of methods

1. Choose a flat surface on which to work. Cover the area with newspapers. Then put a baking tray on the newspapers.

2. Use a hole punch to make a hole near the rim of a plastic container. Attach a spring scale to the container through the hole.

3. Put 230 grams (0.4 pint) of sand in the plastic container. Place it at one end of the baking tray.

Continued

4. Use the spring scale to pull the container with a steady amount of force across the length of the baking tray. Once the container is moving at a steady rate, observe and record the force it takes to keep the container moving. This is your control.

Step 4

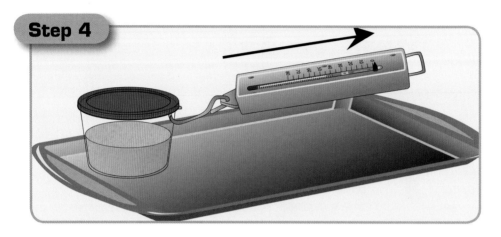

5. Repeat step 4 two times. Take an average of your results by adding the three figures together and then dividing the sum by three (the number of trials that you carried out). Remove the container from the baking tray.

6. Pour 60 millilitres (0.1 pint) of water on the baking tray. Repeat steps 4 and 5.

7. Repeat steps 4 and 5 using 60 millilitres (0.1 pint) of vegetable oil and then using 60 millilitres (0.1 pint) of dish soap. Each time, the liquid should be spread thinly and evenly on the baking tray. Make sure you wash the baking tray thoroughly before each trial.

Step 7

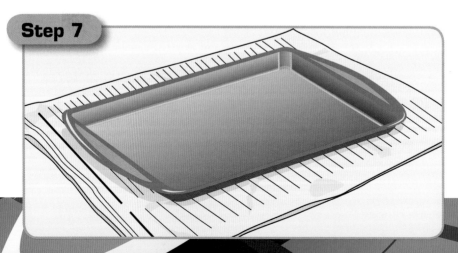

Analysis of results

» Did the force needed to move the container change?

» Which lubricant caused you to use the most force?

» Which lubricant caused you to use the least force?

» Which lubricant reduces friction the best?

More activities to extend your investigation

» Try using different materials as lubricants.

» Try rolling the container of sand over a layer of pencils. Compare the amount of force needed to move the container over the pencils with the amount of force needed to move the container over the lubricants.

» Try cooling the lubricants by putting them in the refrigerator. Repeat the experiment and see how temperature affects the results. Predict what you think would happen if the lubricants were warmed.

» Try adding extra sand to the container and repeat the experiment.

Project extras

» Show your results in both table and graph forms.

» Include photographs of your experiment to show your set-up.

Pulling the container over a layer of pencils may also reduce the friction.

Load it up

Pulleys are a type of **simple machine.** Simple machines give you a **mechanical advantage** – they let you use less force than if you don't use them. You know that pulleys are useful when you need to move something from one height to another, such as raising a flag or raising sails on a mast. Do pulleys make it easier to lift something heavy? Try this experiment if you'd like to find out.

Do your research

Pulleys can be used by themselves or as a group. A pulley that does not move is called a fixed pulley, and one that does move is called a movable pulley. A combination of pulleys working together is called a **block and tackle**. Learn more about these types of pulleys before you begin this project. Once you've done some research, you can try this project. Or, you may come up with your own unique project after you've read and learned more about the topic.

Here are some books and websites you could start with in your research:

» *Machines in Action: Pulleys and Gears*, Angela Royston (Heinemann Library, 2003)
» *Simple Machines: Castle Under Siege!* Andrew Solway (Raintree, 2005).
» Pulley systems: http://www.walter-fendt.de/ph11e/pulleysystem.htm

Background information

Possible question

Does a pulley make it easier to lift a heavy load?

Possible hypothesis

It is easier to lift a heavy load when using a fixed pulley, a movable pulley, or a combination of pulleys.

Level of difficulty	Approximate cost of materials
Advanced	£10.00

Materials needed

» Thin-**gauge** rope or string, 150 centimetres (60 inches) long

Materials needed (cont.)

» A weight or mass, such as a fishing sinker, that weighs about 200 grams (7 ounces)
» A spring scale that measures to 5 newtons
» Two chairs
» A broom handle
» Masking tape
» Two pulleys – one of the pulleys must have two places to which you can tie string or connect an eye hook (Pulleys can be purchased at a hardware shop, or you could ask your science teacher whether the school has any you could borrow.)
» Two short pieces of string or two eye hooks (You will use these to attach the pulley to the broom handle.)

» Pulleys: http://www.flying-pig.co.uk/mechanisms/pages/pulley.html
» How stuff works: How a block and tackle works: http://science.howstuffworks.com/pulley.htm

Outline of methods

1. Tie one end of a 150-centimetre (60-inch) string to a sinker. Tie the other end of the string to a spring scale. Hold the spring scale and lift the sinker up. Observe and record the force needed to lift it. This is your control.

Continued

2. Set up a fixed pulley:
   a. Rest the broom handle on two chairs and tape it in place.
   b. Attach the pulley to the handle using either a short piece of string or an eye hook.
   c. Tie one end of the long string to the sinker. Loop the string through the pulley.
   d. Tie the other end of the string to the spring scale.

Step 3

3. Pull the spring scale down to lift the sinker. Observe and record the force needed to lift the sinker. Untie the string from the sinker and the spring scale, and detach the pulley.

4. Set up a movable pulley:
   a. Tie the long string to the broom handle. Thread the string through the pulley.
   b. Use the short piece of string or the eye hook to attach the sinker to the pulley.
   c. Tie the spring scale to the other end of the long string.

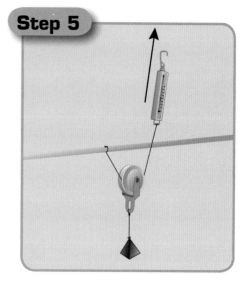

Step 5

5. Pull the spring scale up to lift the sinker. Observe and record the force needed to lift the sinker. Untie the string from the broom and the spring scale. Remove the sinker from the pulley.

6. Set up a block and tackle with one fixed pulley and one movable pulley:
   a. Use the short string or the eye hook to attach the pulley with two attachment points directly to the broom handle. Tie the long string to the other end of that pulley.
   b. Thread the string down around a second pulley, then up and around the top of the first pulley.

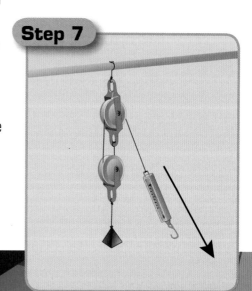

Step 7

    c. Use another short piece of string or an eye hook to attach the sinker to the bottom of the second pulley.

    d. Attach the spring scale to the end of the long string.

7. Make sure there is a gap between the two pulleys. Pull the spring scale down to lift the sinker. Observe and record the force needed to lift the sinker.

Analysis of results

» How much force did each pulley need to lift the sinker?

» Which pulley needed the most effort?

» Which pulley needed the least effort?

» What other factors may have affected the results?

More activities to extend your investigation

» Increase the number of trials used in this experiment. A greater number of trials will increase the accuracy of the results.

» Try adding more pulleys to find out whether that changes the amount of force needed to lift the sinker.

» Try attaching the string and pulleys in different ways to see whether that changes the amount of force you need to apply.

Project extras

» Include photographs of the pulleys you used.

» Show your results in both table and graph forms.

» Include pictures of how pulleys are used in daily life – on flagpoles, in cranes, and on sailing boats.

Get a better lever

What do brooms, seesaws, and bottle openers have in common? They are all simple machines called **levers.** In addition to sweeping, playing, and helping to relieve thirst, levers are useful for lifting heavy loads without using a lot of effort. A car jack is a type of lever that enables you to lift a car with the effort of one arm. How can you construct a lever that best reduces the effort required to move a heavy load? This experiment will help you find out.

Do your research

Levers have two main parts. The rigid rod, or arm, holds the load and receives the effort. The rod pivots on the **fulcrum.** Levers are classified by where the fulcrum, the load, and the effort are located on the arm. Before you begin this project, do some research on the classification of first-, second-, and third-class levers and the mechanical advantage of each type of lever. Once you've done some research, you're ready to begin working on this project. Or, you may come up with your own unique project after you've read and learned more about the topic.

Background information

Possible question

How does moving the fulcrum change a lever?

Possible hypothesis

A lever can lift a heavier load with less effort when the fulcrum is placed closer to the load.

Level of difficulty

Intermediate

Approximate cost of materials

£3.00

Materials needed

» Four elastic bands
» A weight or mass, such as a fishing sinker, that weighs about 200 grams (7 ounces)
» A spring scale that measures to 5 newtons
» A soup or vegetable can
» Corner of a table or work surface
» Two pieces of modelling clay about 4 centimetres (1.5 inches) in diameter
» A metre ruler

Here are some books and websites you could start with in your research:

» *Simple Machines: Castle Under Siege!* Andrew Solway (Raintree, 2005).
» *Simple Machines: Levers*, Sarah Tieck (Buddy Books, 2006).
» Levers: http://www.flying-pig.co.uk/pages/lever.htm
» What is a lever? http://teacher.scholastic.com/dirt/lever/whatlevr.htm
» Types of levers: http://www.teachnetuk.org.uk/2006%20Projects/DT-Mass_Production/MassProduction/Pages/Levers.htm
» NOVA online: Mysteries of the Nile: Lever an obelisk: http://www.pbs.org/wgbh/nova/egypt/raising/lever.html

Outline of methods

1. Loop one elastic band through the top of a sinker. Attach the elastic band to a spring scale. Lift the spring scale. Observe and record the effort needed to lift the sinker. This is your control.

Continued

2. Set up a first-class lever, where the fulcrum is between the effort and the load:

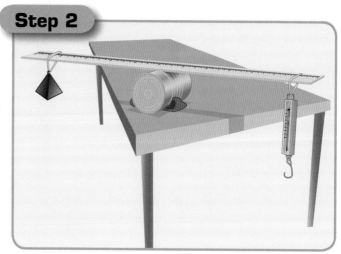

a. Put a can on its side on the corner of a table top. Put a piece of clay on either side of the can to stop it rolling. The can is the fulcrum of your lever.

b. Put a metre ruler so that the 50-centimetre mark is on top of the fulcrum. Make sure the ruler balances on top of the can.

c. Loop an elastic band through the top of the sinker. Attach it to one end of the ruler at the 95-centimetre mark. The sinker is the load.

d. Loop an elastic band through the top of the spring scale. Attach it to the other end of the ruler at the 5-centimetre mark. The spring scale will measure the effort.

3. Lift the sinker by pulling down on the spring scale. Observe and record the effort needed. Repeat this two times. Take an average of your results by adding the three figures and then dividing the sum by three (the number of trials that you carried out).

4. Without moving the sinker or the spring scale, move the ruler so that the fulcrum is at the 25-centimetre mark. Repeat step 3.

5. Repeat step 3 with the fulcrum at 75 centimetres.

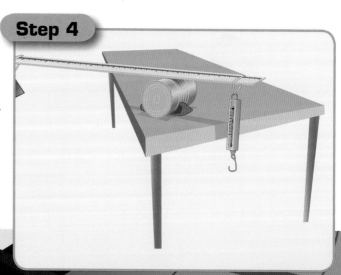

6. Repeat step 3 with the fulcrum at 12.5 centimetres, and then at 87.5 centimetres.

Analysis of results

» How much effort was needed to lift the sinker without the lever?

» How much effort was needed to lift the sinker when the fulcrum was at 50 centimetres?

» How did the amount of effort change when you moved the fulcrum?

More activities to extend your investigation

» Increase the number of trials used in the experiment. A greater number of trials will increase the accuracy of the results.

» Describe how levers are used in everyday life.

» Try the experiment using a second-class lever, where the load is between the fulcrum and the effort. Compare your results.

» Try the experiment using a third-class lever, where the effort is between the load and the fulcrum. Compare your results.

Project extras

» Show your results in both table and graph forms.

» Include photographs of the levers you made.

» Include photographs or pictures of everyday levers, such as seesaws, crowbars, and bottle openers.

» Make a diagram of a first-class lever that shows the placement of the load, effort, and fulcrum.

A shift in gears

If you have a bike with gears on it, you know that changing the gears affects how easy or how hard it is to pedal. How do the gears on your bike work? Why are they different sizes? What is the difference between low gear and high gear? You can complete this experiment to find out.

Do your research

For this experiment, you need a bicycle with at least two gears. If you don't have a bike like that at home, ask whether you can borrow one from a friend or family member. You also need to ask an adult to help you hold up the back end of the bike so that you can turn the pedals without moving the bike. Wear work gloves and old clothes while doing this experiment. You'll handle an oily bike chain, and the oil could get on your hands and clothes.

Before you begin this project, do some research on gears and gear ratios. Once you've done some research, you should be geared up to do this project. Or, you may come up with another project about gears after you've read and learned more about them.

Background information

Possible question

Which gear on a bicycle moves the bike tyre the farthest?

Possible hypothesis

The smallest gear moves the bicycle tyre the farthest.

Level of difficulty

Intermediate

Approximate cost of materials

£3.00

Materials needed

» Two pairs of work gloves
» A bike with at least two gears
» Small, adhesive-backed labels
» String
» A metre ruler
» Adult supervisor

You could start your research with this book and these websites:

» *Machines Inside Machines: Using Pulleys and Gears*, Wendy Sadler (Raintree, 2005)

» How stuff works: Bicycle gears:
http://science.howstuffworks.com/bicycle3.htm

» Simple machines: Clunky cogs:
http://www.sofweb.vic.edu.au/steps/students/5-6years/machines/cogs.htm

» The science of gears: Gear basics:
http://www.fi.edu/time/Journey/Time/Escapements/gearbasics.html

Outline of methods

1. Put on your work gloves. Attach a label to the rim of the bike's back tyre and to each of the gears so that you can observe when each has made one revolution.

Continued

2. Wrap a string around the outside of the back tyre and then measure the length of the string. The measurement is the tyre's circumference. That is the distance the tyre travels in one revolution.

3. Use string in the same way to measure the circumference of each of the bike's gears. To do this, wrap a string around the outside of each of the gears you're going to test.

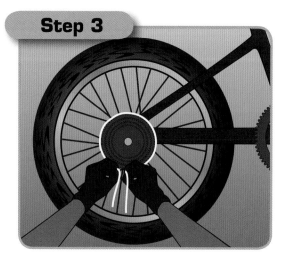

Step 3

ADULT SUPERVISION REQUIRED

4. **Caution: You need an adult to help with this part of the experiment. The adult should wear work gloves.**

Put the bike in first gear. The adult needs to lift the back of the bike while you turn the pedals to get it in gear. Note which of the gears the chain is on. Turn the pedals so the gear rotates once. Observe and record how many times the tyre makes a revolution. When the gear has rotated once, ask the adult to grab the tyre to stop its movement.

Step 4

5. Convert the number of revolutions to the distance travelled by multiplying the number of revolutions by the circumference of the tyre. If it turned a partial revolution, use the string to measure the distance.

6. Repeat steps 4 and 5 with the bike in other gears. For example, if your bike has 10 gears, carry out the experiment in 5th, 7th, and 10th gears.

Analysis of results

» What was the greatest distance the bike tyre travelled?

» What was the shortest distance the bike tyre travelled?

» Which gear caused the tyre to travel the greatest distance?

» Is there a connection between the size of the gear and the distance the bike tyre travelled?

More activities to extend your investigation

» Carry out the experiment several times. A greater number of trials will increase the accuracy of your results.

» Try using a bike with smaller tyres. How does tyre size affect the distance travelled?

» Compare the difficulty of pedalling in each of the gears.

» Describe why bikes with gears are useful.

Project extras

» Include photographs of you doing the experiment.

» Show the results in both table and graph forms.

» Create a poster of your project. Cover paper plates with aluminium foil, or buy disposable aluminium dishes. Cut them out to look like metal bike gears. Decorate your poster with the cut-outs.

Circle work

If you have ever tried to tighten a nut and bolt, you know how useful a wrench can be. It is almost impossible to move the nut with your bare hands. How does a wrench make work easier? Does a longer handle or a shorter handle change the amount of force needed to turn a nut? Try this experiment to find out.

Do your research

In order to do this experiment, you need an adult to help you drill a hole in a piece of wood for a bolt to go through. You also need two wrenches that fit on the nut: one with a short handle and one with a long handle. A wrench is a flat, straight piece of metal, but when it's turning a nut, it works like a wheel and axle. The wrench turns in a circle, like a wheel. It turns around the bolt, which is the axle.

A wheel and axle is one type of simple machine. Before you begin your project, do some research to find out more about simple machines. Once you've done some research, you can work on this project. Or, your research may lead you to develop a different project after you've read and learned more.

Here are some books and websites you could start with in your research:

» *Simple Machines: Castle Under Siege!* Andrew Solway (Raintree, 2005).
» *Wheels: A Pictorial History*, Edwin Tunis (Johns Hopkins University Press, 2002)
» Edheads: Simple machines:
   http://www.edheads.org/activities/simple-machines

Background information

Possible question

Which requires less force to turn a nut on a bolt: a short-handled wrench or a long-handled wrench?

Possible hypothesis

A long-handled wrench requires less force to turn a nut on a bolt than a short-handled wrench does.

Level of difficulty

Intermediate

Approximate cost of materials

£10.00

Materials needed

» A drill
» A block of wood about 10 centimetres (4 inches) square and at least 1 centimetre (0.4 inch) thick
» A bolt about 1 centimetre (0.4 inch) in diameter and at least 5 centimetres (2 inches) long
» A nut that fits the bolt
» Duct tape
» Long-handled wrench that fits the nut
» Spring scale
» Short-handled wrench that fits the nut
» A metre ruler
» Adult supervisor

» What is a wheel and axle?
http://www.sciencetech.technomuses.ca/english/schoolzone/Info_Simple_Machines.cfm

» Simple machines, work, force, and energy:
http://www.sirinet.net/~jgjohnso/simple.html

Outline of methods

1. **Caution: An adult must use the drill.**
   Ask an adult to drill a hole the diameter of the bolt through the block of wood.

Continued

2. Put the bolt through the hole. The bottom of the bolt should stick out of the wood so you can put on the nut and tighten it.

3. Put the nut on the bolt. The nut should be snug but not difficult to move with the wrench. This may take a few tries to determine exactly how tight or loose the nut should be.

4. Place the wood so that it sits on two flat surfaces. There should be a gap between the two flat surfaces. The bolt should point upwards. Use duct tape to secure the wood to the surfaces so it does not move when you loosen the nut.

5. Put the long-handled wrench onto the nut. Attach the spring scale to the end of the wrench by taping the hook in place. The scale should point in the direction you will turn the wrench.

Step 6

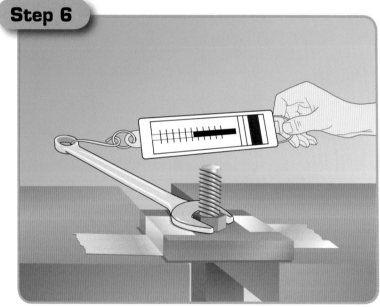

6. Loosen the nut by pulling on the spring scale in one complete circle. Observe and record the force shown on the spring scale as you pull. If the bolt moves while you are loosening the nut, ask your adult assistant to hold the bolt in place.

7. Tighten the nut one full turn with the wrench to return the nut to its original position. Repeat step 6 two times. Take an average of your results by adding the three figures and then dividing the sum by three (the number of trials that you carried out).

8. Put the short-handled wrench on the nut and repeat steps 5 to 7. If you do not have a short-handled wrench, tape the spring scale to the centre of the long-handled wrench.

9. Tape the metre ruler to the long-handled wrench so that the handle is longer than it was before. Tape the spring scale to the far end of the ruler. Repeat the procedures in steps 6 to 7.

Analysis of results

» What was the average force needed for each size wrench?
» Was there a difference in the force needed?
» Which wrench required the least force?
» What other factors may have affected your results?

More activities to extend your investigation

» Describe how a wrench can be classified as a wheel and axle, even though it doesn't look like one.
» Describe how a spring scale works.

Project extras

» Show your results in both table and graph forms.
» Include photographs of your experiment, showing the spring scale's results for each handle.
» Make a poster of your project and decorate it with pictures of bolts and wrenches.

To the top of the mountain

Climbing to the top of a hill takes a great deal of effort, especially if you go straight up. Paths and roads that go up hills and mountains are usually built with a lot of hairpin bends – these roads seem to endlessly travel backwards and forwards as they lead up to the top. The hairpin bends make you travel a greater distance, but do they make it easier to go up the hill? Is there a relationship between the distance and the amount of force it takes? Try this project to find out.

Do your research

In order to do this project, you need a lot of sand to build a model mountain with a road along it. The mountain road or path is actually a simple machine called an **inclined plane,** or **ramp.** Moving an object up an inclined plane is easier than lifting it straight up because the inclined plane allows you to use less force over a greater distance. The angle of an inclined plane is called the **slope** or grade. Before you begin this project, do some research on inclined planes, work, and mechanical advantage. Once you've done some research, you'll be ready to work on this project. Or, you may come up with another project to do after you've read and learned more about the topic.

Here are some books and websites you could start with in your research:

» *What Do Ramps and Wedges Do?* David Glover (Heinemann Library, 2006)
» *Simple Machines: Castle Under Siege!* Andrew Solway (Raintree, 2005)

Background information

Possible question

How does the length of a ramp affect the force needed to move an object up a hill?

Possible hypothesis

It requires more force to move an object up a hill if it has a short, steep ramp than if it has a longer, less steep ramp.

Level of difficulty

Easy

Approximate cost of materials

£3.00

Materials needed

» A sandy place, such as a beach or sandpit
» A spade
» Water to add to the sand to make the sand easier to work with
» A metre ruler
» A spring scale with measurements in newtons
» A toy truck, small enough to lift using the spring scale
» A ball of string
» Scissors

» Simple machines, work, force, and energy:
http://www.sirinet.net/~jgjohnso/simple.html
» The inclined plane:
http://sln.fi.edu/pieces/knox/automaton/plane.htm

Outline of methods

1. Build a hill of damp sand 50 centimetres (20 inches) tall. It should be firm and wide enough to build a road for a toy truck to drive on.

2. Attach a spring scale to the front of the toy truck and lift it straight up into the air. Observe and record your results. (If it requires less than 3 newtons to lift, add weights, such as washers, to the bed of the truck. Otherwise, you won't be able to measure the force needed to pull the truck up the slope.)

Continued

3. Use the spade to make a flat road that goes straight from the bottom to the top of the hill.

4. Place the truck on the road. Use the spring scale to pull it steadily and constantly up to the top of the hill. Observe and record the force needed. Repeat this two times. Average your results by adding the three figures and then dividing the sum by three (the number of trials you carried out).

Step 4

5. Find the length of the straight road by cutting a piece of string to the exact length of the road. Measure the string with the metre ruler.

6. Cut a piece of string that is twice as long as the first string. Using the same starting and ending points, wind the entire length of this string from the bottom to the top of the hill. You need to use at least one hairpin bend. Flatten the sand along this route to make a road.

Step 7

7. Use the spring scale to pull the truck up this winding road. Observe and record the force needed. Repeat this process twice and average your results.

8. Repeat steps 6 and 7 with strings that are three times and four times as long as the original string.

Analysis of results

» How much force was needed to lift the truck straight up in the air?

» How much force did you need to pull the truck up the straight road on the hill?

» How much force did you need to pull the truck up the longer, winding roads with hairpin bends?

» What is the relationship between the length of the road and the force needed to pull the truck?

More activities to extend your investigation

» Try the experiment using a straight ramp made from plywood that is exactly the same length and reaches the same height as the hairpin bend roads you made in the sand. Compare the results.

» Research road building in mountainous areas. Include this information in your report.

» Change the surface of your road by coating it with gravel or small bricks. Compare your results with those you got in your original experiment.

» Scientific work is measured by multiplying force by distance. Calculate and compare the work for each road length that you used. (When you carry out the work calculation using metres and newtons, work will be measured in joules.) Make sure you convert the distance in centimetres into metres before you carry out the calculation. Divide the number of centimetres by 100 to get the distance in metres.

Project extras

» Include photographs of the roads you built.

» Create a poster of your project and include impressive photos of real mountain hairpin bends.

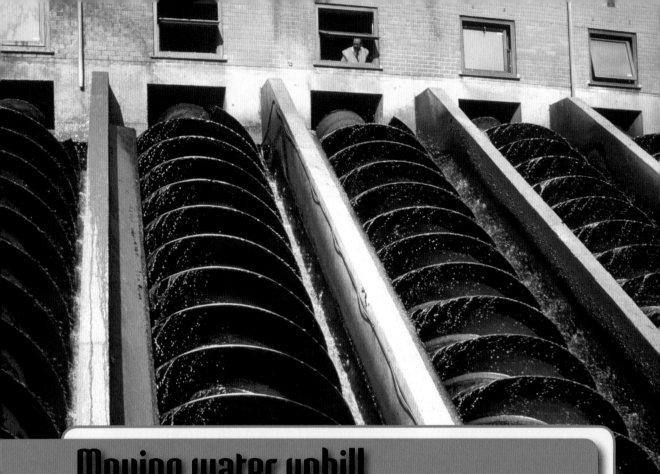

Moving water uphill

One of the oldest machines known to humankind is called the **Archimedes screw.** It was designed to make water move from a lower point to a higher point – something water usually doesn't do. Archimedes screws are still in use today, with only a few changes to the original design. Which design is the most efficient? Which moves the most water with the least effort? Try building a few to find out.

Do your research

The Archimedes screw has the same components as the simple machine called the screw. The screw is actually an inclined plane that circles a central point. Before you begin this project, look at "To the top of the mountain" on pages 28–31 and do some additional research on Archimedes and screws. Once you've done some research, you can dive into this project. Or, you may come up with your own unique project after you've read and learned more about the topic.

Background information

Possible question

Which is the more efficient design of an Archimedes screw: an open one or a closed one?

Possible hypothesis

A closed Archimedes screw is more efficient than an open one.

Level of difficulty

Advanced

Approximate cost of materials

£10.00

Materials needed

» One 100-centimetre (40-inch) length of clear plastic tubing 5 centimetres (2 inches) in diameter

Materials needed (cont.)

» Two PVC pipes, 50 centimetres (20 inches) long and 5 centimetres (2 inches) in diameter (You can purchase pipes at a hardware shop, or you can use a cardboard tube of the same size, waterproofed with duct tape.)
» Masking tape
» A measuring jug
» Water and food colouring
» Two plastic containers or shallow bowls that can hold about 500 millilitres (1 pint) of water
» A stack of blocks about 20 centimetres (8 inches) tall
» A stopwatch
» Four plastic-coated paper plates
» Scissors
» Waterproof tape (Wide parcel tape or duct tape will work.)

You could start your research with this book and these websites:

» *Archimedes: Mathematical Genius of the Ancient World*, Mary Gow (Enslow, 2005)
» Archimedes screw: http://www.tiscali.co.uk/reference/encyclopaedia/hutchinson/m0002929.html
» Simple machines: http://www.fi.edu/qa97/spotlight3 (scroll down to the screw)
» Archimedes screw animation: https://www.math.nyu.edu/~crorres/Archimedes/Screw/ScrewAnimation.html

Continued

1. Make a closed Archimedes screw with plastic tubing. Twist the clear plastic tubing clockwise around the PVC pipe so that it covers the length of the pipe (see illustration for step 5). Tape the ends in place.

2. Pour 300 millilitres (0.5 pint) of water into a plastic container, and place it on a flat surface. To see the movement of the water more easily, add a few drops of food colouring to the water.

Step 5

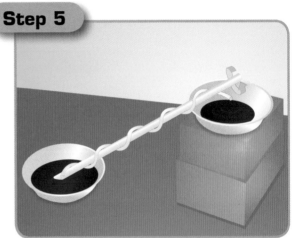

3. Put an empty container on top of a stack of blocks.

4. Position the pipe so one end is in the water and the other end is over the empty bowl on the stack of blocks.

5. Turn the Archimedes screw anticlockwise at a steady rate for two minutes. Measure and record the amount of water that is lifted into the container on top of the stack of blocks.

6. Repeat step 5 two times. Average the results (see page 30 for instructions).

Step 7

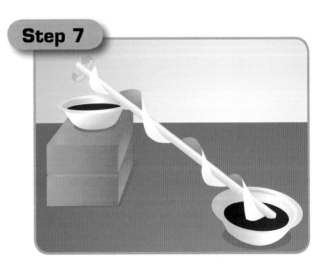

7. Make an open Archimedes screw using the paper plates, waterproof tape, and the second PVC pipe.

   a. Cut a circle from the middle of each of four plastic-coated paper plates so that the rim is 5 centimetres (2 inches) wide. Discard the centre circles. Cut through the rim of each plate.

b. Use the waterproof tape to attach the rims of the plates in a continuous spiral strip around the PVC pipe. Make sure that the rims are connected and well sealed. The strip should wind around the pipe from end to end.

8. Repeat steps 2 to 6 using the open Archimedes screw. Compare the results from both designs.

Analysis of results

» How much water did you lift with the closed screw?
» How much water did you lift with the open screw?
» Which screw design was more efficient?
» What other factors may have affected the results?

More activities to extend your investigation

» Repeat the experiment several times. A greater number of trials will increase the accuracy of the results.
» Try changing a variable in your design, such as the diameter of the tubing or the width of the paper plate. How does that change affect the results?
» Research other ways in which water is lifted without using electrical power.

Project extras

» Show your results in both table and graph forms.
» Include photographs and illustrations of different designs of Archimedes screws.
» Include photographs of your designs.

Hovering around

A hovercraft is a machine for moving across water on a cushion of air. Most hovercraft use an engine to force air under a rubber skirt. The air lifts the hovercraft and propels it forward. This experiment involves making a hovercraft using balloons to force air under a wooden disk. How does changing the shape of the balloons affect the performance of the machine? Try this project if you'd like to find out.

Do your research

You'll use hot glue and a glue gun, or strong wood glue, to construct your hovercraft, so make sure you get an adult to assist you. Before you begin this project, do some research on hovercraft and how they are designed. Once you've done some research, it will be a breeze to work on this project. Or, after you've read and learned more about hovercrafts you might come up with your own unique project to do.

Background information

Possible question

Does changing the design of a hovercraft affect its performance?

Possible hypothesis

Changing the design changes the way a hovercraft moves.

Level of difficulty

Advanced

Approximate cost of materials

£10.00

Materials needed

» A wooden disc, 10 centimetres (4 inches) in diameter – this will be the base of your hovercraft

Materials needed (cont.)

» A drill
» Sandpaper
» A wooden spool (You can purchase spools of thread at a craft shop. Unwind the thread from the spool.)
» Hot glue and glue gun, or a strong wood glue
» 11 round balloons
» 11 long balloons
» A plastic balloon pump
» A metre ruler
» A smooth, flat surface, such as a marble floor or a smooth kitchen work surface, for the race track
» Adult supervisor

You could start your research with this book and these websites:

» *Pull Ahead Books: Hovercraft*, Lisa Bullard (First Avenue Editions, 2007)
» PBS kids: Hovercrafts:
http://pbskids.org/dragonflytv/show/hovercraft.html
» BBC: Science A–Z: Hovercraft:
http://www.bbc.co.uk/norfolk/kids/science/az_hovercraft.shtml
» Technology student: The hovercraft:
http://technologystudent.com/culture1/hover1.htm

Continued

Step 1

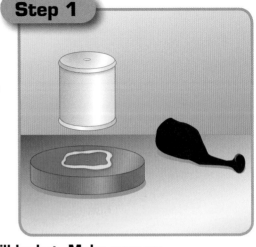

1. Build a hovercraft:

   a. Caution: Ask an adult to use the drill. Drill a hole in the centre of a wooden disc. The hole should be about 5 millimetres (0.2 inch) in diameter.

   ADULT SUPERVISION REQUIRED

   b. Sand one side of the disk so that it is smooth.

   c. Caution: The glue from the glue gun will be hot. Make sure an adult assists you. Do not touch the glue until it has hardened. Work away from small children and pets. Line up the hole in the spool with the hole in the disc and then attach the spool to the unsanded side of the disc with glue. Make sure no glue covers the hole. (Though hot glue works best, you can also use strong wood glue.)

2. Use the pump to determine how much air you can get into both a long and a round balloon. You should be able to get 7 to 10 pumps of air into each. Once you have this information, discard the two balloons – they will be stretched and will affect your results.

3. Pump the predetermined amount of air into a new round balloon. Twist the neck of the balloon and attach it to the top of the spool on your hovercraft.

Step 4

4. Place the hovercraft on a smooth, flat surface and let go of the balloon. Observe and record the distance the hovercraft travels. Discard the balloon.

5. Repeat steps 3 and 4 with the remaining nine round balloons.

6. Repeat steps 3 and 4 with the 10 long balloons.

Analysis of results

» What was the farthest distance the hovercraft travelled with the round balloons?

» What was the average distance the hovercraft travelled with the round balloons? (To find the average, add all of the distances and then divide the sum by the number of trials.)

» What was the farthest distance the hovercraft travelled with the long balloons?

» What was the average distance the hovercraft travelled with the long balloons?

» Which type of balloon caused the hovercraft to travel farther?

» Which type of balloon caused the hovercraft to travel straighter?

» What other factors might have affected the results?

More activities to extend your investigation

» Try changing another part of your hovercraft to see how the change affects the distance or the way the machine travels. For example, instead of a wooden disc, use a small paper plate.

» Add a "skirt" made from a plastic bag to the base of the hovercraft and see how this affects the way that the hovercraft travels.

Project extras

» Show your results in both table and graph forms.

» Include photographs of real hovercraft in your report.

» Include photographs of your hovercraft and how you built it.

Moving from here to there

Design is an important aspect of any machine. When engineers design a boat, for example, they must consider the boat's use, its shape, and the properties of the materials that will be used to build the vessel. This often involves testing several designs to determine which works the best. Do you think you can design and build a fast boat? Try this project and test your boat design skills.

Do your research

You will need to try out your boat designs in a pond, swimming pool, or bath. Make sure you get permission from an adult before going near the water.

You will build a paddle boat for this project. Before you begin, do some research on paddle boats, as well as other boats and their designs. Once you've done some research, you can begin this project. Or, you may come up with your own idea to work on after you've read and learned more about the topic.

Background information

Possible question

Which design element most affects the speed of a paddle boat?

Possible hypothesis

The placement of the paddle affects the speed the most.

Level of difficulty

Intermediate

Approximate cost of materials

£3.00

Materials needed

» Six polystyrene trays (the type you get when you buy fresh meat at the supermarket – the supermarket may give you clean ones if you say they're for school, or you can buy them at a craft shop)
» Scissors
» A metre ruler
» Elastic bands
» A stapler and staples
» A pool of water
» A stopwatch, or a watch with a second hand

You could start your research with this book and these websites:

» *The Amazing Book of Paper Boats*, Jerry Roberts (Melcher Media, 2006)
» OMSI engineer it! Water: http://www.omsi.edu/visit/physics/engineerit/water.cfm
(click on Paddleboats, Sailboats, and Online Games)
» Paddle steamer animation: http://www.bbc.co.uk/history/interactive/animations/paddlesteamer/index.shtml

Outline of methods

1. Use one polystyrene tray to build your control model:
   a. Cut the front of the tray to form a triangle, with the sides cut at approximately 45-degree angles.

Continued

b. Cut a 12.5-centimetre (5-inch) by 10-centimetre (4-inch) rectangle from the back of the boat.

c. Cut 5 millimetres (0.2 inch) from each side of the rectangle. Cut the rectangle into two pieces, 4 centimetres (1.6 inches) from the front end. The narrowest rectangle is the paddle wheel.

Step 1a–c

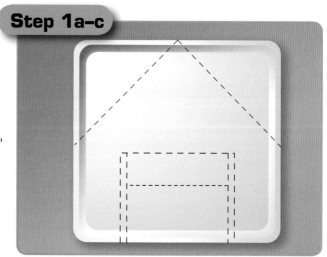

d. Staple an elastic band across the centre of the paddle wheel.

e. Staple each end of the elastic band across the centre of the rectangular hole you cut out. Use three or four staples on each side.

Step 1d–e

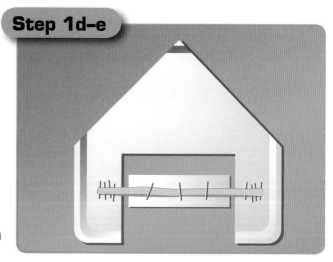

2. Mark off 100 centimetres (40 inches) in your pool of water.

3. Twist the elastic band 50 times. (You might need to increase or decrease the number of turns, depending on the thickness of your elastic band.) Hold the band in position so that it doesn't untwist.

4. Put the boat in the water at one end of the pool. Release the propeller so that the elastic band can untwist. Observe and record the time it takes for the boat to move 100 centimetres (40 inches).

5. Repeat steps 3 to 4 two times. Take an average of the results by adding the three figures and then dividing the sum by three (the number of trials that you carried out).

6. Build another boat, changing one element of your original (control) design. Repeat steps 3 to 5. Here are four ways to change your design.

You can choose from these changes or come up with your own. Just make sure you change only one design feature at a time.

» Build the boat with a rounded front rather than a pointed one.
» Attach the paddle in a different place, either closer to the front or farther back.
» Change the size of the paddle.
» Change the thickness of the elastic band.

Analysis of results

» What were the results of each design trial?
» Which design produced the fastest speed?
» Which design produced the slowest speed?
» What other factors may have affected your results?

More activities to extend your investigation

» Repeat the trials for each design several times and average your results. A greater number of trials will increase the accuracy of the results.
» Build another type of boat, such as a sailing boat, and compare your sailing boat results with your paddle boat results.

Project extras

» Show your results in both table and graph forms.
» Include photographs of the different paddle boat designs you made.
» Show photographs of actual paddle boats in your report.

Writing your report

In many ways, writing the report of your investigation is the hardest part. You've researched the science involved, and you've had fun gathering all your evidence together. Now you have to explain what it's all about.

You are the expert

Very few other people, if any, will have done your investigation. So you are the expert here. You need to explain your ideas clearly. Scientists get their most important investigations published in a scientific magazine or journal. They may also stand up at meetings and tell other scientists what they have found. Or they may display a large poster to explain their investigation. You might consider giving a talk or making a poster about your investigation, too. But however scientists present their investigations, they always write it down first – and you must too. Here are some tips about what you should include in your report.

Some hints for collecting your results

» **Making a table:** Tables are great for recording lots of results. Use a pencil and ruler to draw your table lines, or make a table using a word processing program. Put the units (m, s, kg, N and so on) in the headings only. Don't write them into the main body of your table. Try to make your table fit one side of paper. If you need two sheets of paper, make sure you write the column headings on the second sheet as well.

» **Recording your results:** It is often easy to forget to write down your results as they come in. Or you might just scribble them onto the back of your hand, and then wash your hands! A wise scientist will always make a neat, blank table in their lab book before starting. They will write down their results as they go along and not later on.

» **Odd stuff:** If something goes wrong, make a note of it. This will remind you which results might not be reliable.

» **Precision:** Always record your readings to the precision of your measuring equipment. For example, if you have scales that show 24.6 g, don't write 24 or 25 in your table. Instead, write 24.6 because that's the precise measurement.

Laying out your report

You could use the following headings to organise your report in a clear manner:

» A title
This gives an idea of what your investigation is about.

» Aims
Write a brief outline of what you were trying to do. It should include the question you were trying to answer.

» Hypothesis
This is your scientific prediction of what will happen in your investigation. Include notes from your research to explain why you think your prediction will work out. It might help to write it out as: "I think … will happen because …"

» Materials
List the equipment you used to carry out your experiments. Also say what any measuring equipment was for. For example, "scales (to weigh the objects)".

» Methods
Explain what you actually did in your investigation.

» Results
Record your results, readings, and observations clearly.

» Conclusions
Explain how closely your results fitted your hypothesis. You can find out more about this on the next page.

» Bibliography
List the books, articles, websites or other resources you used in your research.

And finally ... the conclusions

There are two main bits to your conclusions. These are the "Analysis" and the "Evaluation". In the analysis you explain what your evidence shows, and how it supports or disproves your hypothesis. In the evaluation, you discuss the quality of your results and their reliability, and how successful your methods were.

Your analysis

You need to study your evidence to see if there is a relationship between the variables in your investigation. This can be difficult to spot in a table, so it is a good idea to draw a graph. You should always put the dependent variable on the vertical axis, and the independent variable on the horizontal axis. The type of graph you need to draw depends on the type of variables involved:

» A bar chart if the results are **categoric**, such as hot/cold, male/female.

» A line graph or a scattergram if both variables are **continuous**, such as time, length, or mass.

Remember to label the axes to say what each one shows, and the unit used. For example, "time in s" or "height in cm". Draw a line or curve of best fit if you can.

Explain what your graph shows. Remember that the reader needs help from you to understand your investigation. Even if you have spotted a pattern, don't assume that your reader has. Tell them. For example, "My graph shows that the paddle boat travelled faster than the sailing boat." Circle any points on your graph that seem anomalous (too high or too low).

Your evaluation

Did your investigation go well, or did it go badly? Was your evidence good enough for you to support or disprove your hypothesis? Sometimes it can be difficult for you to answer these questions. But it is really important that you try. Scientists always look back at their investigations. They want to know if they could improve their methods next time. They also want to know if their evidence is reliable and valid. Reliable evidence can be repeated with pretty much the same results. Valid evidence is reliable, and it should answer the question you asked in the first place. As before, remember that you are the person who knows your investigation the best. Don't be afraid to show off valid evidence. And be honest if it's not!

Glossary

accurate close to the true value

Archimedes screw device used to move water uphill

block and tackle system of two or more pulleys

categoric variable that can be given labels, such as male/female

continuous variable that can have any value, such as weight or length

control something that is left unchanged in order to compare results against it

data factual information

effort force or energy applied to do work

evidence data that has been checked to see if it is valid

friction force that keeps an object from moving

fulcrum point on a lever around which the lever pivots

gauge measurement of thickness

hypothesis scientific idea about how something works, before the idea has been tested

inclined plane simple machine that is a sloped surface

lever simple machine made from a rigid bar that pivots at one point to lift a load

lubricant material used to reduce friction

mechanical advantage difference between the effort applied and the resulting work

newton unit of force

prediction say in advance what you think will happen, based on scientific study

ramp inclined plane

simple machine tool used to make work easier

slope angle of incline

variable something that can change; is not set or fixed

work force making an object move through a distance

Index